Untamed illusions

Karthik Krishnamoorthy

Presentation by *BookLeaf Publishing*

Web: www.bookleafpub.com

E-mail: info@bookleafpub.com

ISBN: 9789357743969

First edition 2023

ACKNOWLEDGEMENT

I would like to sincerely thank my literature and language teachers from both Gokuldham High School as well as Prabhavati Padamshi Soni International Junior College, for shaping my thoughts and encouraging me to express them freely. I'm deeply thankful to "Buddy" (Aparna Balwally) who helped me unleash my creativity in literature. I greatly appreciate the team of Bookleaf Publishing for bringing this book to life for me. Last but not least I'm grateful to my best friend Prithvi Unni who has tirelessly worked on many of the illustrations in this book.

And yes, thank you and love you family!

INDEX

A Man Against An Army

© Prithvi Unni

Lighting the way in this gloomy domain
his presence with us is the only hope now;
A might so overwhelming he went unrivaled
the allies now had reason to cheer out loud

He stood there alone facing an army,
his godly power against the blood-craving
enemies;
The only chance we have, the chances of a slim
victory
It rests in his hands, it rests in his abilities

One ray of hope,
the one light that's burning,
we helped our savior through all of the turnings,
A wounded savior, now fallen on his knees
The bloodthirsty enemies now declared him
deceased

It wasn't time for mourning it was our last
chance, a last push we all gave,
supporters of freedom against the crazy
dictators,
in one swift motion the light was extinguished,
the world now filled with craters and craters

Tears

Generated using Bing Image Creator

If tears could convey what we've all wanted to
say
Oceans and rivers and lakes beyond vales
Containing the sadness or the depths of our
happiness
It would continue filling up until the end of our
days

Tears of sorrow or tears of glee
Tears of relief from the bodies of the free
There isn't much we can do to stop the filling of
the seas
After all it's filled with the tears of our
memories

In the end all we could taste was the sorrow
Filling up the world as if there were no morrow
The flavor of pain slowly spreading through the
oceans
The flavor of hope now receding into the depths
Stirring the world into a state of unrest

And so, we stand at the edge of this vast
expanse,
Where tears have flowed, both in joy and in
pain,
In the depths of these waters, our emotions
dance,
Leaving behind imprints, like a permanent stain.

Rebuilding Hopes

Amidst the sound of guns and big bombs,
Innocent lives are taken, families are torn.
The horrors of war, far beyond our imaginations,
Damage stretching across countries from station
to station.

Battles fought for power and greed,
they all leave behind wounds that never will
recede.
The cries of the wounded and the dying,
Echos heard through the land, echoes of endless
crying

After the war is over its always a haunting sight,
the people have stopped hoping for a future
bright;
shattered buildings lay still there catching dust,
the lives of people are now just empty husks.

But life doesn't end here and people started to
think,
how to make this world better and not let it sink;
Through brotherhood and companionship they
all picked it up,
This is how they walked the war off with a
strut...

Troubled Appearance, Distorted Mind

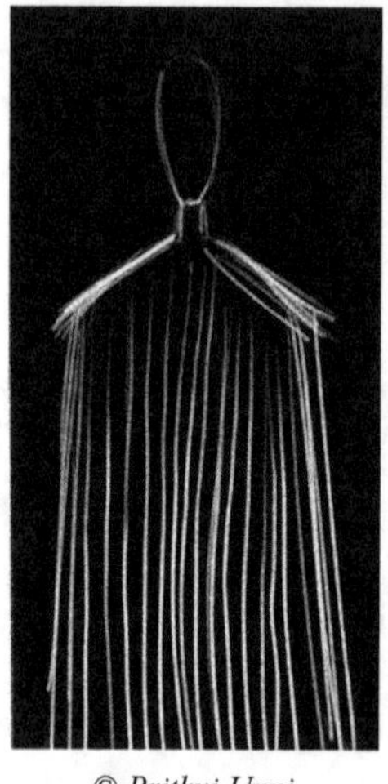

© Prithvi Unni

The glass allowing me to see clearly,
an appearance I have never seen before in my
life;
What I've shown to the rest of the world so
dearly,
stabbed me in the back like a knife.

A dark silhouette with a gloomy aura,
walking around with no aim at all;
I realized now how I've been feeling,
I realized I couldn't stand tall.

Lost in the shadows of my own creation,
I search for a glimmer of light;
But the path ahead offers no salvation,
Only echoes of my internal fight.

In this labyrinth of doubts and fears,
I stumble upon fragments of my past;
The mistakes, the regrets, the unshed tears,
Haunting me, as if they were meant to last.

Yet within this chaos, a whisper of hope,
A seed of resilience takes root;
I gather my strength, learning to cope,
Embracing the lessons life will impute.

With each step forward, I reclaim my might,
Rebuilding the fragments, piece by piece;
The glass may shatter but I know I'll shine
bright,
For my spirit's strength will never cease.

So now I rise, a phoenix from the ash,
With newfound purpose and a heart unbound;
I'll forge my own destiny, from the shattered
pieces of the glass,
Guided by the courage that I have found.

Paranoia

© Prithvi Unni

Our resting lives made unrest
Signs of the troubled past keep beating in my
chest
Surviving this wilderness as if it's a test
After declining the behest of sadness
Here comes paranoia, it's tryna destroy ya

Tip Toeing its way into my life
This looming shadow, outlined by the moon
Hearing our hearts pounding in the room
you can just feel it's your doom
Is it just a weak attempt for a quick ticket to the
afterlife

Or our atrocious nightmares, present in the
room.
This paranoia makes me feel paralyzed.

An inch away from death we are, and still
instilling fear
The bloodlust of paranoia corrupting the people
near.
Whether its knives to the heart
Or your precious hard work fall apart
You falling through an elevator shaft
Or just drowning in a river all because of an
overturned raft
Remember!
We live here to conquer. Paranoia? pfft! consider
it conquered.

It's always that one feeling
That it is watching, it is killing
But I'm done with this world of injustice
It's time to break free
Oh paranoia, be gone thee!

Death and death

Till death do us part,
are the words spoken while making an
everlasting bond,
until they do meet Death,
they never thought they would be alone.

With no gender and no name,
Death lurks around the wide world;
From house to house like a beast untamed,
taking adults from children, young from the old.

Separating the soul from the body with its
scythe,
nobody dares challenge Death even with all their
might;
although death for any living being is inevitable,
Death is unstoppable

Although we can't cheat death,
Death can be cheated,
anywhere everywhere wherever you are seated,
Death can't touch you under the bright light
that's heated.

The sun is our protector,
its light is what we must use;
To keep Death far far away,
Until we reach the end of the line,
the long line of our fate.

Freedom

Generated using Bing Image Creator

Like the never-ending storms present in the
ocean,
strikes on and on throughout our lives;
A downer to our hopes and dreams,
A drag to our hopes to be free.

After falling deep down, looking through a
one-sided glass;
I saw myself, myself devoid of the shackles that
hold us back,
My free self basking in the happy sun's reign,
My careless self neglecting the future, playing
the present world's game.

Days and nights of merriment which I then
hadn't the slightest clue that I would repent;
Throughout the years I slowly transformed,
A free bird to a caged one, to one who has
forgotten all,
to one who has forgotten to sing, forgotten how
it felt to fly
forgotten the free bird's call.

Bound by the shackles limiting me to this form,
as the appearance of the endless ocean's surface;
Guilt and anger-like emotions forming the
waves,
Marooning the deep seabed of freedom,
Freedom from the shackles of life.

Goodbye Brother

Rivers filled with tears,
each drop, a memory;
They knew they realized their worst fears,
the fear of losing each other.

Happy ones, sad ones all ran down their cheeks,
filling glasses to its brims,
mountains to its peaks.

Could not be apart,
cannot be separated,
such was the bond between two brothers.

Despite being a thousand miles away,
it was not hard to hear;
The sounds of them crying,
crying for each other.

A Tear During War

A single tear rolling down the cheek,
multiple languages it can speak;
falling so gently with utmost grace,
one of the only common things among the
human race.

Sometimes it's a tear of joy, a tear of pure
delight,
A moment so beautiful, it always shines so
bright;
Other times it's a tear of pain, of deep sorrow,
A heartache that pierces, with no sight of
tomorrow.

Tears for the wounded, tears for the hurt,
tears for your loved ones who have now mixed
with the dirt;
As those who go to war most never return,
this is how the world, it will slowly burn.

Tears of sadness, the only thing keeping the
world from burning,
dousing the fire with its pain and remorse;
Safe to say there is a learning,
we should make war change its course.

Yet Another Sea Gone

Generated using Bing Image Creator

With the seas green crystal and clear,
all the fishes, seals and otters they cheer,
swimming around the great oceans with
absolutely no fear,
No one knew that soon enough there would be
tears.

The whales and sharks all lived peacefully,
swimming under the moon and the sun;
This undisturbed cycle of harmony,
was unfortunately not a long-lasting one.

Soon enough bodies washed up on the shores,
black waters killing even more and more;
Falling debris hitting tunas and sharks,
the little ones couldn't survive anymore.

When the fog cleared hundreds were dead,
to the destroyed ships and boats they were fed,
red ones and white ones all fishes turned up
dead,
all the big problems were human-led.

Plastics and wastes disgracing the world;
Schools of fish became singular students,
quietly silencing animals herd by herd,
it's only the scale of all these pollutants.

The sea even with all its might and glory,
powerless to act against all this tyranny;
We used to hear the voices of animals
unanimous,
now all of the voices have seized;
It is too late to know that we are the disease,
we are the reason they lost their peace.

Racism

In shadows of the world, a haunting tale,
Racism's venom spreads, a bitter gale.
Boundaries of hate, cutting deep and wide,
Humanity weeps, men, women and children hide

From distant lands to lands unknown,
The seeds of racism are grudgingly sown.
Colors of skin, a target of scorn,
Discrimination, humanity's thorn.

In streets of despair, cries echo loud,
Prejudice dances in an arrogant shroud.
Brothers and sisters, united by grace,
Yearning for acceptance, a warm embrace

In classrooms where dreams should brightly
soar,
Bias lurks, hearts tremble, spirits roar.
Knowledge undivided, wisdom untold,
Yet racism's chains, so painfully bold

Through generations, wounds have bled,
But resilience rises, a force widespread.
Hands held together, hearts intertwined,
Only through love for each other, the cure we
can find.

The Bridge of Transcendence

Generated using Dreamer

Where the river of existence meanders wide,
A bridge emerges, stretching far and wide.
Its arches a symbol, connecting realms
unknown,
Where life converges with death's solemn
throne.

One side adorned in hues of vibrant mirth,
A bustling world that celebrates birth.
Laughter echoes, and dreams take flight,
As souls dance under the sun's golden light.

But beyond the bridge's midpoint, a subtle
change,
A transition where shadows grow, dark and
strange.
Whispers of eternity, a somber refrain,
The other side beckons with an ethereal domain.

Across the span, life's footsteps softly tread,
Seeking solace in the whispers of the dead.
Each step, a surrender to the great unknown,
Leaving behind the familiar, to paths unshown.

The bridge, a threshold, a passage unbound,
Where the veil is lifted, where answers are
found.
A bittersweet journey through the river's divide,
Guided by faith, with hope as a faithful guide.

And as we traverse, memories in our wake,
We glimpse the essence of life's fragile ache.
For in the union of life and death's embrace,
We find a truth that transcends time and space.

The bridge, a symbol of our mortal quest,
A testament to the souls who never rest.
Through its embrace, a profound understanding,
That life's continuum lies in death's
commanding.

So let us tread, with hearts steadfast and strong,
On the bridge that binds us, where we belong.
For in crossing over, we discover our worth,
Embracing the cycle, the eternal rebirth.

Animals in the Crossfire

Withering leaves from enchanted forests,
destruction and chaos spreading,
all because the two nations couldn't just be
honest,
the hopeless animals lay there dreading.

The days to come they would never know,
one day to survive it's hard to show,
grasping at the last straws to protect their home,
these days are tough, it's an all-time low.

A fight between two nations,
the innocents caught in the crossfire,
because they gave in to their temptations,
the animals are in a situation dire.

With no power to save themselves,
the innocent ones will die,
we all wish they could save themselves,
we all want them to survive.

Another world's mistake they are facing,
the brunt of the impact is everlasting,
it's all because two other worlds fighting,
the animals are now just grasping,

grasping for a twig to survive,
grasping for a tiny bit of air they hope they
won't die

If I Were God

Generated using Bing Image Creator

If I were God, with powers untold,
A universe in my hands, a story to unfold,
I'd paint the skies with hues all divine,
A celestial canvas, a masterpiece, so fine.

I'd pluck the stars from the cosmos and
rearrange their glow,
Creating constellations in patterns that
conspicuously always shows
The tales of mortals, their triumphs and strife,
A cosmic tapestry, the fabric of life.

I'd mend the broken hearts, heal every wound,
Restore faith and hope, where it seemed
marooned,
I'd wipe away tears, replacing them with wide
smiles,
Unveiling grace and love across countless miles.

If I were God, the mountains I'd shape,
Carving majestic peaks, a grandiose landscape,
I'd sculpt the valleys, gentle and serene,
A sanctuary of peace, where souls convene.

The oceans would dance to my every command,
Tides rising and falling, as I weave the sand,
I'd breathe life into rivers, flowing free,
Nourishing the earth, a lifeline for all to see.

I'd walk among the creatures, however great or
small,
Bestowing harmony, ensuring that they never
fall,
Their vibrant colors, melodies in the air,
A symphony of creation, a world beyond
compare.

If I were God, I'd light a flame within each soul,
A spark of divinity, making each one completely
whole,
I'd inspire dreams and help ignite a sacred fire,
Guiding humanity towards love's infinite desire.

But in my heart, I'd remember still,
That even as God, I'd hold a humble will,
For true power lies not in ruling from above,
But in serving others with boundless love.

Unchangeable Fates

Writing our own fates,
before they unfold,
it's such a sight,
such a story to be told.

Good or bad,
bitter or sweet,
there's nothing we can do except,
live it on repeat.

Reliving the good ones twice,
in the end we all know that it just won't suffice,
it has a way of pulling us, a way to entice,
into knowing our fates more than we can bite.

Then the bad ones show,
don't feel like you want to live it again anymore,
in writing it was bad enough,
but living it would be just way too tough.

More people ending this inevitable suffering,
not realizing the extent of their mistake,
it wasn't meant to be their ending,
as the loved ones cry for their sake.

The Con-Man

Generated using Bing Image Creator

All the stories that he foretold,
to the young ones and old ones he had sold,
with all the people flocking towards him,
he made chests and treasuries full of gold.

Nobody knew his power lay in thinking,
so in his quick money scheme they all went
down sinking,
all their money, heart and soul selling
to this Entrepreneur, to this person with a mind
scheming

Selfish he was as a person,
this unjust practice he continued rehearsing,
with people of no mind of their own,
getting trapped in his own cage sewn.

Slowly they all come to realize,
that they couldn't understand,
they were blinded even with all eyes,
the intention behind this cruel master plan.

A Soldier's Sacrifice

A world in chaos, a battlefield of pain,
Where wounds run deep and the element of
chaos reigns,
The sound of gunfire echoes through the land,
As soldiers fight for what they believe, they all
take a stand.

Families wrecked, homes destroyed,
Innocent lives lost, more soldiers deployed,
As the battle rages on with no end in sight,
The defenders of the country scream with all
their might.

Amidst the chaos, hope still survives,
As they now fight on, with valor in their eyes,
Their sacrifice, a reminder of the cost of peace,
That war may bring victory, but never true
release.

A World In Ruins

Generated using Bing Image Creator

There are no winners in war
Soldiers everywhere are now all the way up
there,
spectating the battle with god,
win or lose the outcomes are never fair.

New holes tearing across the world,
as each mighty nation goes against another;
The large waters are now disturbed,
as people swim far away for cover.

From country to country, continent to continent,
all the people try and flee,
while the nobles sit at home with their heart and
soul content,
the people know not when there would be hope
for glee.

A war-torn world has nothing to give,
but pain and suffering and the corpse's hum;
If war continues to live
the whole world will come undone.

The Pursuit of Happiness

© Prithvi Unni

Writing without it,
I can't help but think about it;
All those good things that I thought I would
write about,
Has all been bad memories with no easy way
out.

Writing about happiness and of closure,
While I only know how little I had composure;
Keeping the truth away from people at all costs,
I hope I knew what to write, I've never been so
lost.

False hopes and anger filling up inside of me,
I guessed that my happy memories are outside of me,
me,
It isn't fair, I'm so used to this that I don't care.

Negative stuff is not the only thing to write about,
about,
I'm trying to find the bright side on my way out;
It's not easy it's a journey we must all make,
In the pursuit of happiness, we must make memories to take.

A Teenager's Saga

To shine on and forget all those troubles I have
had
I've longed for that seclusion, always as a lad,
I'm done with its pressure always keeping me
sad
If this doesn't get over I know I'll be driven mad

Exams, Entrances, Extracurriculars and whatnot
captured our young childhoods for which we all
fought
all of my happiness over all the years since birth,
they suddenly seemed like a dot,
a dot somewhere in the big and sad plain of hurt

Upsetting to see such little happy memories,
I decided to take it up on me,
I finally knew it's time to break free,
I'm done with letting my past completely tire
me.

The Mask

© Prithvi Unni

Trying to pretend no matter what,
I can't defend even if I want.
These emotions of mine piling on top of each
other,
it's further ahead, it's more than it's ever been.

Putting on a mask in front of people,
cloaking my emotions with a tough barrier,
all this so they don't know the truth
people could call me a coward, but I'd say I'm a
warrior.

It isn't easy pretending,
it could ruin my chances of a happy ending,
secluding these thoughts, these thoughts from
everybody else
it's just me, only me and no one else.

A smile so they don't know,
hope I'll be happier when further along I go;
Slowly friends and family left,
deserted I now felt alone;
the cost of putting on the mask I realized,
is more than I would ever know.

www.ingramcontent.com/pod-product-compliance
Lightning Source LLC
La Vergne TN
LVHW051241200726
843510LV00011B/1636